T0360002

DID YOU KNOW?
Koala

DID YOU KNOW?

Koala

young reed

Contents

What is a Koala?

● Koalas are **mammals** that belong to the **marsupial** family, alongside animals such as kangaroos and possums. Young marsupials live in their mother's **pouch**.

● The Koala is the only living member of the family Phascolarctidae. The species' scientific name — *Phascolarctos cinereus* — means '**grey pouched bear**'.

Wombats are the Koala's closest relative.

● Although Koalas do look a bit like a bear, the two animals are not closely related.

● Today, the Koala's closest relatives are the ground-living **wombats**.

- Koalas have a long **oval-shaped nose,** dense **grey fur** and **no tail.**

- The name Koala is derived from the word *gula,* which in the Dharug language means **'no drink'.** Koalas do not need to drink as they get enough water from their food.

- Koalas are **nocturnal,** meaning that they are more active at night and often sleep during the day.

Special adaptations

- Koalas are **arboreal**, meaning that they live mostly in trees.

- Their long sharp **claws** help them to climb trunks and branches.

- They have **opposable thumbs** to help them grab on to trees and their food.

Where do Koalas live?

● Today, captive Koalas are a familiar sight in **zoos** and **animal parks** around the world, where they have become a favourite attraction for millions of people.

● In the wild, however, Koalas live only in **eucalyptus forests** in **eastern Australia**.

Territory matters

- The area of a Koala's territory varies greatly — from **one square kilometre** to more than **one hundred square kilometres** — depending on how much food is available.

● Although they live mostly in trees, Koalas will sometimes walk on the ground for long distances in search of new habitat.

● A male Koala will proclaim its territory with a loud **grunting** or **bellowing noise**.

What's for dinner?

- **Eucalyptus leaves** — Koalas need to eat lots of them to get enough nutrients.

- Koalas only eat **fresh new eucalyptus shoots**.

- A Koala's body can process and **remove toxic chemicals** from the leaves.

● Because of the large amount of leaves eaten, Koalas produce a **lot of poo** – up to **two hundred** small pellets each day.

• Once too big for the pouch, the joey will often **hitch a lift** on its mother's back.

Family life

● Just like a kangaroo, a baby Koala is called a **joey**.

● A joey is only **two centimetres long** when it is born. It immediately climbs through its mum's fur and into a **pouch** to feed on **milk**.

● Larger joeys **feed on a special type of poo** provided by mum, which consists of chewed-up and partly digested eucalyptus leaves. **Yummy!**

Threats to Koalas

- Today the Koala is listed as **Endangered** and its population is decreasing.

- Most of the biggest threats to the existence of Koalas come from **humans**, including habitat loss, introduced predators, road traffic accidents and bush fires.

● Monitor lizards, Powerful Owls and Dingos are among the Koala's natural predators.

Conserving Koalas

- All of us need to do more to **protect Koala habitat**.

- If you own a **dog**, you can help! Do not take dogs to places where there are Koalas — the presence of dogs in their habitat is very dangerous and stressful for them.

● Luckily there are many kind people who have set up **animal hospitals** and **rescue centres** to help injured or orphaned Koalas.

First published in 2025 by
New Holland Publishers
Sydney

newhollandpublishers.com

Level 1, 178 Fox Valley Road, Wahroonga, NSW 2076, Australia

Copyright © 2025 New Holland Publishers
Copyright © 2025 in images: Shutterstock.com

A record of this book is held at the National Library of Australia.

ISBN 978 1 92107 387 8

OTHER TITLES IN THE 'DID YOU KNOW?' SERIES:

Kangaroos
ISBN 978 1 92107 386 1

Meerkat
ISBN 978 1 92107 389 2

Lizards
ISBN 978 1 92107 388 5

Penguins
ISBN 978 1 92107 390 8

Red Panda
ISBN 978 1 92107 391 5

For details of these books and hundreds of other Natural History titles see newhollandpublishers.com